J.K. ROWLING'S
Wizarding World™

Movie
MAGIC

✦ VOLUME 2 ✦

J.K. ROWLING'S
Wizarding World™

Movie
MAGIC

VOLUME 2

Curious Creatures

Ramin Zahed

WALKER
BOOKS

An Insight Editions Book

CONTENTS

Introduction

One of the most thrilling parts of watching the eight Harry Potter movies and *Fantastic Beasts and Where to Find Them* is seeing the extraordinary creatures envisioned by author J.K. Rowling come to life on the big screen. Many teams of concept artists, visual effects artists, model-makers and computer graphics professionals worked hand in hand with the production designer, directors and producers to create believable creatures that seem at home in the wizarding world.

Production Designer

Production designers are responsible for creating the environments seen in a film, including the designs of the sets and shooting locations. In addition, production designers oversee the art department and concept artists. Stuart Craig has been the brilliant production designer for all of the Harry Potter films as well as *Fantastic Beasts and Where to Find Them*.

> "The beasts may be inspired by animals we all know and have seen before, but they are also creatures that are completely out of this world and fantastic in every way."
> —Stuart Craig, Production Designer

Concept Artist

Concept artists are given the job of envisioning what characters, props and environments in a film should look like. Working closely with the production designer, visual effects supervisors, directors and producers, concept artists for the wizarding world movies come up with informative sketches and illustrations of the various creatures. They often look at animals in the real world as well as illustrations of mythical creatures for inspiration.

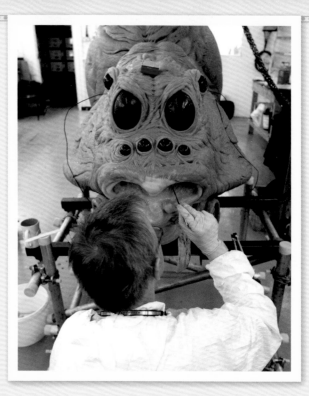

Creature Shop Artist

In the early Harry Potter movies, the best way to produce otherworldly creatures such as Buckbeak and Aragog was to build them! The creature shop created life-size animatronic versions that could be manipulated on set. For other creatures such as the dragons, physical models were built and then scanned digitally for the visual effects department to work with. Creature shop artists are often talented artists, sculptors, and model-makers who know exactly what kind of material to use to deliver the most believable magical beasts.

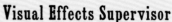

Visual Effects Supervisor

Each of the films had at least one visual effects supervisor, whose job it is to work with the director, production designer and cameraman to bring the magical images we see in the finished movies to life. They make sure the creatures and environments that are added digitally blend in perfectly with the live-action footage shot in the studio or on location and work closely with the film-makers to make sure their vision is brought to life. In the earlier movies, each creature had to be built as a sculpture or maquette and then scanned digitally. With advances in technology, visual effects artists now use tools such as ZBrush software to create the creatures directly with computers.

PART I

FANTASTIC BEASTS

AND WHERE TO FIND THEM

NEWT'S MAGICAL CASE

Newt Scamander learns a tough lesson early on in the movie. Never lose sight of your magical case! After all, this magical carrier may look like any old brown leather case, but it has the special ability to contain all the fantastic beasts *and* their habitats. Bewitched with an Undetectable Extension Charm, this amazing case is much, much bigger on the inside than the outside. It also has an enchanted lock so Newt can hide the contents from No-Majs (that's the American term for people without magical skills or abilities) and Muggles, which comes in handy when he has to pass through customs in New York City.

"The whole place was created by Newt himself, so it has this homemade, do-it-yourself look. It seems crude at first, but more magical and seemingly endless the further you explore."
—Stuart Craig, Production Designer

An Incident at the Bank

The Niffler is a major player in the unfortunate case switch that takes place near the bank. The creature escapes from Newt's case and wreaks havoc in the bank, which is filled with the sort of shiny objects that it loves. To help the actors interact with the Niffler realistically, the production team built a puppet as a stand-in. In postproduction, the visual effects artists swapped out the puppet for the animated digital version to bring the creature to life.

A Distracted Little Creature

The Niffler is a clever creature that is always on the lookout for shiny objects, but he's also easily distracted. "He hasn't yet finished with one thing when he sees the next object of desire," says concept artist Rob Bliss. "He's quite distracted in that sense. The purse felt like a funny prop to show his absolute focus and interest as he wrestles to retrieve its contents. As the clasp gives way, the money pops out, and his heart skips a beat as the coins shoot out ahead of him."

"Newt and the Niffler have this wonderful love–hate relationship... He causes a lot of chaos, but I kind of love to hate him." —Eddie Redmayne (Newt Scamander)

Bowtruckle

Bowtruckles are tiny green sprig-like creatures that can easily blend into any leafy background. No taller than eight inches and peaceful in nature, Bowtruckles are known to eat insects and act as tree guardians. They look like tree stems with roots, leafy branches and two small brown dots for eyes. They come in very handy for picking locks!

Odd Bowtruckle Out
In addition to the shy Pickett, who prefers to stay in Newt's jacket pocket, there are other Bowtruckles in Newt's magical case. Unlike Pickett, Titus, Finn, Poppy, Marlow and Tom prefer to live in a tree.

Take ... zoo?

Bowtruckles were one of the hardest creatures to design. According to the visual effects team, more than two hundred designs were created before the final version of the creature got the green light. "The Bowtruckle was difficult because twig men have been done before and there are only so many permutations to joining sticks together to form a figure," says concept artist Paul Catling. "For this reason, I initially resisted going down the twig route and took inspiration from insects that try to mimic their environments. In the end it was thought that it would be impossible to inject enough cuteness into an insect to allow it to rummage around Newt's ears!"

"Pickett has attachment issues. Newt knows he shouldn't have favourites, but he loves Pickett to sit in his jacket pocket anyway. I fell for him quite badly."
—Eddie Redmayne
(Newt Scamander)

"This Bonsai tree, home to the Bowtruckle, was designed by Dermot Power and later crafted by the propmaking team. It's so beautiful, but completely artificial!"
—Stuart Craig, Production Designer

ERUMPENT

A giant mammal with a playful nature, the Erumpent's closest real-world cousin is the rhinoceros. The enormous African beast has a glowing horn, a heavily armoured hide capable of repelling most spells and charms, and a tail that resembles a long rope. Its sharp horn contains a poisonous fluid that causes anything it pierces to explode. Newt's Erumpent is a female and is desperately seeking a mate – which has some funny implications when she falls for Jacob Kowalski!

Erumpent

Class B
Tradeable Material
thick hide
repells most curses & charms.

Contains deadly fluid,
causes whatever it
injects to explode

Can be used in
potions

Horn will glow before
explosive agent is released

Single horn /
rope-like tail

HABITAT & TERRAIN CODES		
NO		Aquatic / Amphibious
NO		Burrowing
NO		Desert
YES		Tropical/Equatorial ✓
YES		Temperate ✓

TM & © WBEI. (s17)

How to Seduce an Erumpent

Though the Erumpent was animated digitally, the film-makers felt it was important that actor Eddie Redmayne have something to act with on set when it came time to perform a complicated mating dance. "We brought in a team of experienced puppeteers to operate an enormous wireframe Erumpent puppet we built," explains visual effects supervisor Tim Burke. "She didn't have a face, but the puppeteers gave the Erumpent such realistic movements that Eddie was able to react to her and perform the dance wonderfully to lure her back into the case."

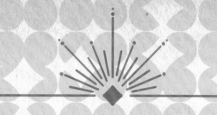

Demiguise

A native of the Far East, this gentle primate-like creature looks like a silver-haired orangutan with large, thoughtful brown eyes. It can become invisible whenever it wishes to and it is able to predict the immediate future. That's why the only way to capture it is to do something totally unpredictable and unexpected. Its long silky hair is quite sought after and is used to make Invisibility Cloaks in the wizarding world.

The Demiguise and the Occamy share a habitat inside Newt's case.

Imitating Professor Slughorn

Director David Yates told the visual effects team to study the movements and facial gestures of actor Jim Broadbent, who played Professor Horace Slughorn in *Harry Potter and the Half-Blood Prince*, as a reference for the Demiguise.

Riding on Jacob's Shoulders

For a scene in which the Demiguise climbs on the back of Jacob Kowalski (played by Dan Fogler), the visual effects team used a technique called rotoscoping, which combines two elements in a live-action scene to be composited against a background. In the final version, the creature seems to be getting a piggyback ride from Jacob.

Occamy

Is the Occamy a snake, a dragon, or a bird of paradise? Maybe it's a little bit of all three. Covered in layers of beautiful feathers, this native of the Far East and India has a serpentine body, two legs and wings. It is also *choranaptyxic*, which means it grows or shrinks depending on the space it occupies. The Occamy egg is made of pure silver and is quite precious. In the movie, the Occamy chicks are protected by the Demiguise, who acts as their patient babysitter.

OCCAMY HABITAT

A Work in Progress

The Occamy was one of the most difficult creatures to design, because its visual qualities weren't completely defined in the beginning. "It could have been anything, so evolving a design was harder," says concept artist Rob Bliss. "Sometimes the constraints do the designing for you."

From Silver to Blue

The Occamy egg went through several design and colour changes. The art department knew that the inside had to be silver, and the original idea was to make the exterior silver as well. However, the designers played with different shades of silver and light blue to match the colouring of the adult Occamy. They added some patterns and enamel finishes to evoke the script's description of a valuable yet soft silver shell. The final version looks like a palm-size duck egg with a weathered, organic feel – but the egg's valuable interior remains pure silver.

THUNDERBIRD

A native of the deserts of Arizona, the Thunderbird is a large, eagle-like bird. It has multiple sets of powerful wings and can actually cause a storm by flapping them. Newt rescued his Thunderbird from the clutches of traffickers in Egypt and named him Frank. He promised the bird that he would return him to his original habitat in Arizona. Years of being kept in chains had taken their toll on the once-captive bird, evidenced by the scars on his legs. At the end of the movie, Newt releases Frank into New York City. With help from Newt and a vial of Swooping Evil venom, the Thunderbird creates a storm to Obliviate the city's No-Majs.

An Appaloosa Excuse
Though Newt has come to the United States to set Frank free, he makes sure he has something else he can tell authorities, which is that he's searching for a rare Appaloosa Puffskein!

THUNDERBIRD HABITAT

Please Excuse My Storm

The Thunderbird had to look majestic and iconic. Adding extra wings definitely helped to distinguish it from other birds, but the artists wanted something more striking, and found inspiration in the bird's name itself. As it flies through the sky, it is able to generate wild thunderstorms from its large wings. Its feathers darken, just like storm clouds, as it releases its energy.

SWOOPING EVIL

Imagine if a mad scientist had crossed a giant reptile and a huge butterfly with colourful, spiked wings. The result would probably look a lot like the Swooping Evil. This strange and beautiful creature has the power to suck the brains out of its enemies' heads. When it's not active, it lives in a spiny green cocoon.

Manta Ray to the Rescue

To come up with the design of the Swooping Evil, the artists studied natural reference material, including video footage of the manta ray. This sea creature inspired the way the Swooping Evil ripples and rolls its wings. The artists also examined the details and movements of bats and birds. The Swooping Evil was designed to feel graceful and powerful at the same time.

The Swooping Evil's venom, if properly diluted, can be used to help remove bad memories.

Fwooper

An African bird with orange, pink, lime-green or yellow feathers, the Fwooper is an exotic creature known for its fantastic plumage and dazzling, patterned eggs.

Beauty in the Details

The design of the Fwooper was based on specific illustrations from concept artist Paul Catling, so the visual effects team had less development research work to do. However, creating the bird's feathers wasn't easy. The visual effects artists had to groom the feathers to match Paul's artwork, taking into consideration how the Fwooper would fly, land and even fluff itself! They learned a lot in the process, even if the Fwooper is just a small creature.

Pink Feathers

The final version of the Fwooper is pink and looks a little like an owl, and the visual effects team actually used the physical details of an owl's feathers and patterns to make sure their exotic bird looked natural.

BILLYWIG

A vivid blue insect native to Australia, the Billywig is about a centimetre long. Because of its amazing speed, it's rarely noticed by No-Majs. The Billywig's wings are attached to the top of its head and it has a long, thin stinger at the bottom of its body. When stung by a Billywig, the victim experiences giddiness, followed by levitation.

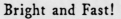

Bright and Fast!

Video footage of dragonflies, beetles and hummingbirds helped the visual artists conjure up their final version of the Billywig. They also observed propeller planes in flight to picture the way the Billywig speeds up so quickly in the air.

Everywhere You Look

Sharp-eyed fans will find several instances of the speedy little escaped Billywig photobombing the camera throughout *Fantastic Beasts and Where to Find Them*.

Murtlap

The Murtlap is a small, hairless, guinea pig–like creature found in coastal areas. It has a peculiar growth on its back that resembles a sea anemone. A wizard or witch who is bitten by a Murtlap might get an itchy rash and a minor resistance to curses and jinxes. Some people are extra sensitive to the Murtlap's bite and suffer much more embarrassing symptoms.

"It was odd how easily the seemingly incompatible mating of a bald guinea pig and a sea anemone came together to look so homogenous!" —Paul Catling, Concept Artist

Doing Their Homework

The film-makers wanted to make sure that the odd-looking Murtlap resembled a very strange animal that might be found near the beach. They looked at as much real-life footage of guinea pigs and sea anemones as they could get their hands on to get the visuals just right. The Murtlap's skin is pinkish and translucent, like that of a hairless guinea pig, and the artists then added the anemone-like tendrils to its back.

DIRICAWL

This plump dodo-like bird has the magical ability to disappear and reappear somewhere else (similar to how wizards can apparate and disapparate) to escape danger. It has fluffy feathers, very short legs, and can't fly. In the film, we see a mother Diricawl and her chicks running through several shots, magically teleporting when they sense danger.

To create this magical bird, the visual effects team made use of reference images of ostriches and emus. They also decided to make the feathers on the Diricawl's body look a bit damaged, but kept the feathers on the head and the crest looking crisp and clean. The result is a fun, imbalanced quality that matches the creature's personality.

DUNG BEETLE

The Dung Beetle featured in the movie is a specific variety of scarab beetle, which is known for living at least partially on fecal matter (aka poo!). Interestingly enough, this beetle was considered sacred by the ancient Egyptians, who associated the beetle's great ball of dung with the sun.

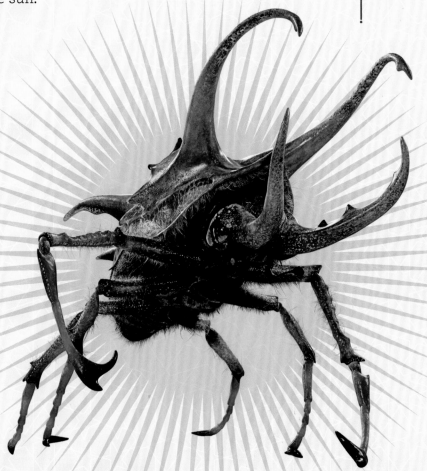

Adding a Touch of Magic
The visual effects team worked to add a more fantastical feel to the Dung Beetle originally designed by concept artists. As a result, the film's Dung Beetles have big horns and transparent parts on the outside of their shells, which are gold in colour.

Poo Art
The visual effects artists who worked on the Dung Beetle had to create piles and sculptures of dung in the environment they built for the creature. It was somebody's job just to create the dung sculptures, and they had to spend a lot of time looking at the reference material!

but
us.
ach,
y in
ed

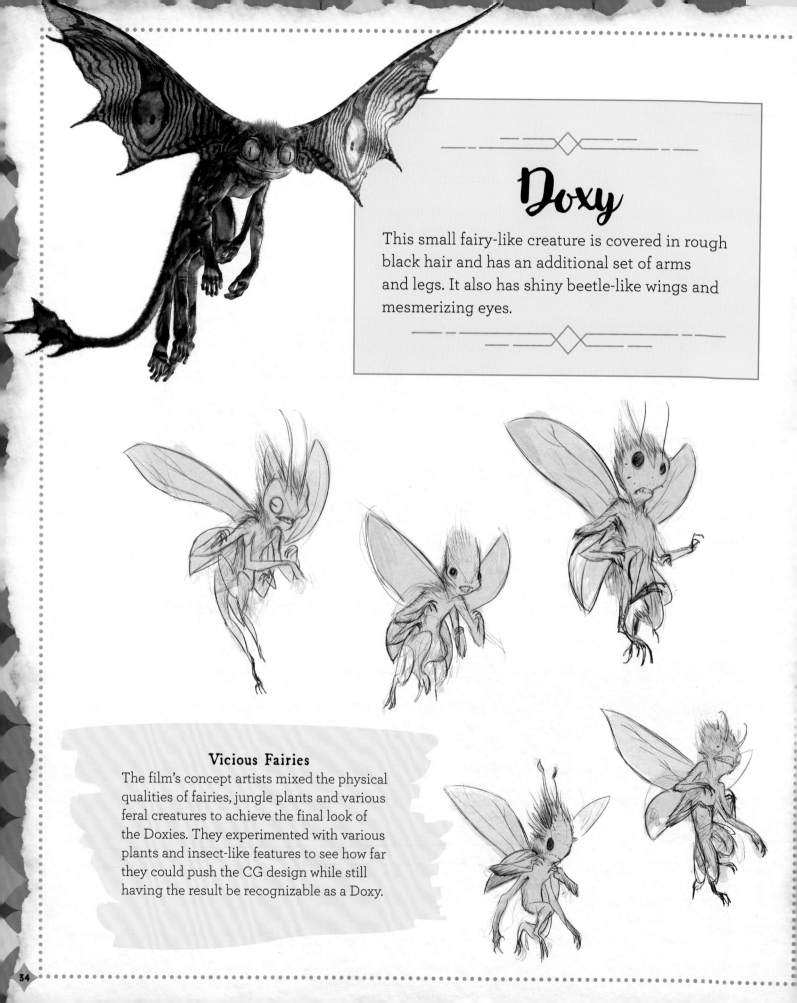

Doxy

This small fairy-like creature is covered in rough black hair and has an additional set of arms and legs. It also has shiny beetle-like wings and mesmerizing eyes.

Vicious Fairies

The film's concept artists mixed the physical qualities of fairies, jungle plants and various feral creatures to achieve the final look of the Doxies. They experimented with various plants and insect-like features to see how far they could push the CG design while still having the result be recognizable as a Doxy.

MOONCALF

Mooncalves are shy mammals that only come out when the moon is full. They have smooth, pale grey bodies with big bulging eyes on top of their heads and four thin, wobbly legs. Their dung acts as a super fertilizer if it is collected before sunrise and spread on magical herb and flowerbeds. Mooncalves are reportedly found all over the world.

Eyes on the Sky

The concept artists who worked on the Mooncalf needed to find a way to make its eyes look natural. "It was described as having eyes on top of its head, which gives the notion that the Mooncalf had somehow evolved solely to stare at the moon," says concept artist Paul Catling.

Skeletons That Fit

In developing the Mooncalf, the artists looked at skeletal drawings of similar creatures, especially sea lions, for inspiration. They had to come up with CG bodies that would look realistic and not overly cartoon-like. The Mooncalf's skeletal features needed to balance the body, so that the creature's movements would seem natural.

MOONCALF HABITAT

The Truth About Mooncalf Poo

When designing magical creatures, artists also had to consider the natural bodily functions of the animals. They even considered the habits and poo size of the Mooncalves when creating their habitat. The droppings had to be the right size and have the right texture, and they had to be distributed correctly along the ground. These poo pats were deposited when the beasts came out at night to stare at the full moon. The surface of the dung is pitted and irregular, kind of like the craters of the moon.

Nundu

A leopard-like mammal, the Nundu is considered one of the most dangerous creatures alive. Its disease-riddled breath is so toxic that it can destroy entire villages of people.

Make It Scary

To express how dangerous the Nundu is, the artists referenced drawings of the hoods worn by medieval executioners as well as the bodies of hairless beasts. They also looked at the way spitting cobras and puffer fish expand when they are threatened and adapted that movement for the creature's lion-like mane, which puffs up when it roars.

Rotten to the Core

Because the Nundu has toxic breath, the visual effects artists decided to look at rotting objects to find inspiration for the Nundu's physical characteristics. The film's concept artists had fun researching some disgusting reference materials – like mange and flesh-eating bacteria.

GRAPHORN

Once found in the mountains of Europe, the Graphorn is a large, aggressive creature with a humped back. Unfortunately, there is only one breeding pair of Graphorns left in existence. Thankfully, they're safe in the hands of Newt Scamander, and they even have babies!

A Fierce Design

"For me, without a doubt the most challenging creature to design was the Graphorn," says concept artist Paul Catling. "I wanted the Graphorn to be absolutely formidable, a huge muscular fore-end but with a flexible, cheetah-like rear that could accelerate impossibly, propelling its horn into its enemy. To feed its vast body, I gave it tendrils around its mouth that could penetrate and instantly devour whole colonies of termites." Paul's intimidating design was refined by the visual effects team, who altered the creature's purple colouration to better match its desert habitat and redesigned the Graphorn's head.

A Family Affair

The visual effects team was tasked with creating an entire family of Graphorns for the movie – a mother, father and two babies. They also had to make sure there was consistency to each design, so the Graphorns felt like a real family. The Graphorns had to feel intimidating at first, but also endearing and nurturing, with strong family bonds. The visual effects team also studied reference art of lions and rhinos to help them instil the animated Graphorns with subtle feelings of weight and heft.

Crocs, Elephants, Rhinos and Caterpillars

For the Graphorn's skin, the visual effects artists looked at crocodiles, elephants and rhinos. The ostrich was the inspiration for the creature's feet. Finally, it was visual effects supervisor Christian Manz who came up with the idea of using a type of caterpillar known as the hickory horned devil as a model for the animal's horns.

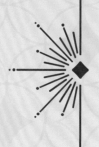

GOBLINS

The unique era and setting of the story gave the artists the chance to show how the goblins of the wizarding world would dress up for a wild night out in the fashionable Jazz Age.

Gnarlak

Gnarlak the goblin is a grumpy gangster who runs The Blind Pig, a magical speakeasy. Similar to some of the other goblins in the Harry Potter movies, Gnarlak is not overly fond of wizards!

"The Blind Pig is filled with a broad range of unsavoury types, but Gnarlak is the most unsavoury of all!"
—Ron Perlman (Gnarlak)

Motion-Capture Magic

To create the goblin, the film's visual effects artists relied on motion-capture technology. Dobby the house-elf was brought to life using the same technology in the Harry Potter movies. Performed by actor Ron Perlman, Gnarlak was created by placing registration dots on the actor's face and then taking pictures of him using one hundred cameras at the same time. All that photographic information about the actor's facial expressions was assembled into the final character image.

Regular Faces

The house-elves who work in the bar and in the MACUSA lobby were designed around interesting-looking people the artists came across in their daily lives. The subjects were photographed; then the artists played around with the images by enlarging and shrinking certain features, making sure that the underlying facial structures remained believable.

Humour Comes to the Rescue

In a scene that didn't make it into the final version of the movie, one goblin had to handle the wind and bass sections of The Blind Pig band all by himself. As concept artist Rob Bliss recalls, "It led to a really funny character sweating it and puffing away on a lot of instruments. This wouldn't have come about had we been allowed more goblins onstage. Sometimes characters or places kind of design themselves, and if humour is appropriate or allowed, then it's helpful when the outcome is a bit absurd. Humour makes things easier!"

The Obscurus

One of the most difficult challenges facing the concept artists and CG wizards working on the movie was visualizing the Obscurus. This is the terrifying, otherworldly entity that has taken over Credence Barebone (played by Ezra Miller) in the movie.

Changing Face

The film's concept artists set out to create a series of images that show how Credence transforms into the Obscurus. The guide was designed to depict this shape-shifting force taking over Credence until his human shape is difficult to discern. Another test borrowed Credence's facial features in an abstract way, using a base sculpt of Ezra. The visual effects artists took sound data from the actor's performance to create CG effects using Houdini, a popular 3-D animation software.

The concept artists had the idea that the Obscurus would always be moving between a gas, a liquid, or a solid state. Mostly vague, there would only be hints of a face or a limb moving around in the dark mass.

"The Obscurus is about rage and anger," explains visual effects supervisor Tim Burke. "It's an incredibly powerful energy force. Later, however, it becomes a beautiful sculpture–like piece of art, swirling and mesmerizing."

Home of the Force

Many early studies of the Obscurus depicted it as something that is barely tangible, but oozing with power and evil. Director David Yates and author J.K. Rowling had thought of it being kept in a glass enclosure or a small vial. Artists also entertained the idea of it being contained in a more organic case that hinted at what was kept inside. It was essential to show how this entity represents the sadness and anguish of the tormented souls it possesses.

Dark Mass

How do you create an invisible monster? That's the question that the concept artists had to answer when they sat down to work out what this shapeless villain would look like and how it would take over Credence's body and soul. Some early ideas described this evil force as an ectoplasmic mass that would surround the afflicted person, eventually growing and taking control of the person trapped inside.

PART II

Harry Potter™

FOREST DWELLERS

CENTAURS

Familiar figures in Greek and Roman mythology, centaurs are magical creatures that have the body of a horse and the torso, head and arms of a man. Harry Potter first encounters the centaur Firenze in *Harry Potter and the Philosopher's Stone* while serving detention in the Forbidden Forest.

Maquettes helped Daniel Radcliffe and the other actors have something centaur-sized to interact with during filming.

Mixing Magic and Mythology

The artists who created the centaurs did a lot of research and referenced classic drawings of the creatures from ancient Rome and Greece. Still, they thought it was important that the centaurs look unique, and not like humanized horses or animalized men. That's why their faces are long with broad foreheads and flat cheeks, noses and jawlines. Their eyes are also set further apart than humans' eyes are, and they have pointed ears set high on their heads. Lastly, they have horse pelt and colouring all over their bodies, not just the bottom half.

Digital Dilemmas

Centaurs also play a major role in *Harry Potter and the Order of the Phoenix*. Unlike Firenze, who was created entirely digitally, full-size models were used to make the centaurs Bane and Magorian. These realistic models created by the creature shop are called maquettes and were used to cyberscan (create and store computer digital versions of) the centaurs into the computer.

The Mane Attraction

The costume and prop teams had to "flock" the centaur models. They covered the entire model with glue and then sent an electrical charge through it. Then they fired oppositely charged hairs at the model so that the hairs would stick to the surface and stand on end.

The Right Direction

The crew had only forty minutes to comb the hair in the correct direction before the glue dried. It took a team of six people to do this, making sure the correct hair colours and combinations were used for the centaurs.

Overall, it took the costume and prop departments (with a crew of more than forty people) eight months to create the centaurs, with all their handcrafted weapons and jewels, from start to finish.

Acromantula

Acromantulas are giant spiders often found in the dense rain forests of Southeast Asia. They have eight black eyes and are usually covered with thick, dark hair.

"I remember the first shot we did in the Forbidden Forest," says Daniel Radcliffe. "Rupert and I walked over this ledge, and suddenly there's a gigantic spider waiting for us. It was so realistic, we were genuinely terrified."

ARAGOG

Hagrid's spider friend, Aragog, made his first appearance in *Harry Potter and the Chamber of Secrets*. A full-grown Acromantula, Aragog is the size of an elephant, with each of his legs almost six metres long. At first, the visual effects team assumed they would have to use computer animation to create the creature. Eventually, the creature shop realized that building Aragog and having him walk and talk on a life-size scale would be a better option.

Hairy Details

room bristles were used for Aragog's finer airs, and feathers (coated with fluff and Lurex, type of yarn woven with metallic threads) ere used for the thicker ones. The hairs were dded one at a time, so you can imagine how ard the creature shop had to work to make the pider's fuzzy features look just right.

Finding Waldo

To make the spider's movements look realistic, the designers used a system called aquatronics, which uses cables pumped with water. Thanks to aquatronics, Aragog's movements were smooth and life-like. His back legs were operated by puppeteers, while the front legs were mechanical. A device called a Waldo was used by a puppeteer to control Aragog's movements and make him move in a sneaky, menacing way, just like a spider.

Burying an Old Friend

A much older version of Aragog was created for *Harry Potter and the Half-Blood Prince*. Because Aragog dies in this movie, the creature makers used a clear material called urethane to give it a special glow. This gave the model a see-through quality, which is similar to how some spiders look when they die in the natural world. The spider also needed to be much heavier in this movie, because it had to slide into a grave on a hill. The film's creature makers became very attached to the magnificent spider. Many of the cast and crew members were teary-eyed watching the scene in the movie when Aragog died and was buried.

BUCKBEAK THE HIPPOGRIFF

Considered by many to be one of the most beautiful and magical creatures in the Harry Potter world, Buckbeak has the front legs, wings and head of a giant eagle, and the body, hind legs and tail of a horse. Buckbeak was first introduced in Hagrid's Care of Magical Creatures class in *Harry Potter and the Prisoner of Azkaban*.

Winging the Right Proportions

For inspiration, the creature designers studied the flight of birds and the trotting motions of horses. Veterinarians and other experts also provided tips on the ideal size of Buckbeak's wings. One of the most challenging parts of the job was creating smooth transitions and motions for the eight-metre-long wings as they went from a wide-open position to fully folded.

Four Times the Fun

Four different versions of the creature were created by the film's designers. Three were life-size models: one was a standing Buckbeak used for foreground shots, another was a freestanding Buckbeak for background shots, and the third was a sitting version that was kept in the pumpkin patch behind Hagrid's hut. The fourth was completely computer-generated and used whenever the magical creature needed to walk or fly.

Feathers and Horsehair

To make sure the three Hippogriffs looked exactly alike, the creature makers used the same kinds of feathers for the bird parts, and similar horsehairs for the lower parts of the animal. As was done with Aragog, the hairs were inserted one at a time to create more realistic models.

THESTRALS

First seen in *Harry Potter and the Order of the Phoenix*, the Thestral is a mysterious, gentle creature. It has the skeletal body of a horse, bat-like wings and two small horns on top of its head.

The Thestral sculpture featured a special jointed back and articulated movements so that the actors could respond naturally when flying on the horse-like creature.

Giant Wings

Although the Thestrals were created digitally, the creature shop assembled a full-scale model to make sure its giant nine-metre-long leathery wings would fit into the Forbidden Forest movie set. This realistic model was then scanned digitally for the computer artists to work on.

Stepping Out of the Shadows

One of the toughest aspects of creating the Thestral was its colour, because it's very difficult to film black objects. That's why the model was painted paler than originally planned. The patchy colours gave the beast an interesting appearance, which made it stand out in the darker shadows of the set.

Poor Starving Creatures

Because the Thestral also had to look extremely thin, the computer animators created a detailed skeleton for the creature. They had to pay close attention so that its thin skin wouldn't get pulled into its bones.

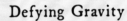

To make the Thestrals more life-like, designers had the beasts flick flies away from their bodies with their tails, just like horses do.

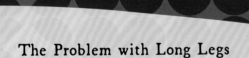

Defying Gravity

In the scenes that featured the Thestral in flight, the visual effects artists had to make the creature's spine longer than it was in the original version. (The Thestral carries only one passenger in *Harry Potter and the Order of the Phoenix*, while two people ride on it in *Harry Potter and the Deathly Hallows – Part 1*.) To create the illusion of flight, the visual effects team used a mixture of aerial cinematography and actors filmed riding the midsection of the Thestral against a blue screen.

The Problem with Long Legs

Another challenging scene was the one in which Luna Lovegood (Evanna Lynch) feeds the Thestral foal in the forest. The creature's long legs and short neck made it difficult for its head to touch the ground. The digital artists took their cue from nature: they had the Thestral spread its legs like a giraffe in order to reach Luna's treats.

LAKE DWELLERS

Merpeople

The haunting merpeople of the black lake oversee the second task of the Triwizard Tournament in *Harry Potter and the Goblet of Fire*. The visual effects experts used a combination of carefully crafted maquettes and computer animation to bring the strange half-human, half-fish creatures to cinematic life.

Merpeople have parallel rows of turtle-like horny plates that run down their backs and along their scaly skin.

You Look Vaguely Familiar

If you look carefully at the physical characteristics of the merpeople, you can see that the creature designers combined human features with those of a sturgeon (especially the eyes and mouth). The merpeople's hair was specifically designed to float underwater like sea anemones – brightly coloured animals that look like flowers and stick to rocks and corals.

Unlike many mermaids seen in live-action and animated movies, these lake creatures have tails that move from side to side, rather than up and down. They also have dorsal and pelvic fins that help them stay balanced as they swim underwater. Their scary piranha-like teeth come in handy when they're fighting other predators or hunting for food.

GRINDYLOWS

The merpeople aren't the only scary black lake residents that make a big impression in *Harry Potter and the Goblet of Fire*. Grindylows are the wicked water-dwelling creatures that were described by the film's creature shop team as a cross between "a nasty child and an octopus".

Big Mouths and Sharp Teeth

The designers came up with many versions of Grindylows at the beginning of the creative process. Some had small heads, while others had huge glowing eyes, webbed feet and large pointy ears. Some looked like frogs; others were shiny fish-like creatures. There were even some that had frog-like bodies, while others looked more like seals and mermaids. Finally, the team decided to pick a design that matched what the creature had to do in the film. That's why the final version of the water demon has a large grinning mouth filled with sharp teeth and powerful octopus-like arms capable of gripping a daring Triwizard champion.

Making Lots of Mischief

The creature shop produced full-size silicone models of the Grindylows. Then they cast them as fibreglass models, which were scanned digitally for the CGI artists. Special computer software was also used to help create a large group of Grindylows quickly and accurately.

Pulling Harry in Different Directions

In one of the many memorable scenes from *Harry Potter and the Goblet of Fire*, Grindylows pull and claw at Harry Potter in the lake. To shoot this scene, two stuntmen acted as stand-ins for the creatures, tugging at Harry's legs in a green-screen underwater tank. Green screens are used during filming so that actors can be placed against a digital background after the scene is shot.

DRAGONS

The motto of Hogwarts school is *Draco dormiens nunquam titillandus* (that's Latin for "Never tickle a sleeping dragon"), and the large-winged, fire-breathing reptiles make frequent appearances in Harry Potter's universe. The variety and colourful details of the dragons allowed the designers and visual effects artists to let their imaginations run wild.

Norwegian Ridgeback

In *Harry Potter and the Philosopher's Stone*, Hagrid (Robbie Coltrane) wins a dragon egg that hatches into a wobbly, shiny, greyish-green baby Norwegian Ridgeback. Hagrid names it Norbert.

An Awkward Baby

The film-makers decided that the baby dragon's body wouldn't be quite developed. Like many baby animals, its head and legs would be larger in proportion to its body than a fully grown dragon's. Even the "ridgeback" that the dragon is known for wouldn't come into its own quite yet.

Digital Dragonet

Norbert was a one hundred percent digital creation. The flames that shoot out of his mouth – and burn Hagrid's beard – were also complete CGI creations.

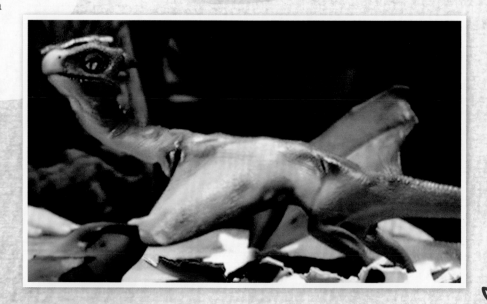

HUNGARIAN HORNTAIL

The concept artists did a lot of homework before coming up with the intimidating Hungarian Horntail dragon guarding the golden egg during the first task of the Triwizard Tournament. This giant reptile had to be different and more fearsome than other dragons the audience had seen in movies and on TV. The designers came up with a wide variety of choices by combining the facial features of rhinos, snakes, lizards and tortoises. They even used the face of an angry Doberman Pinscher for inspiration.

SKY DWELLERS
Designing the Dragons of Harry Potter

Birds of a Feather

...way the Horntail moves in *Harry* ...*blet of Fire*, you'll understand why ...died the movements of falcons, ...(known as predatory birds) for ...Horntail's wings could be animated ...m the rest of its body.

UKRAINIAN IRONBELLY

We encounter the Ukrainian Ironbelly in the lowest level of Gringotts in *Harry Potter and the Deathly Hallows – Part 2*. This particular dragon has been held captive by the goblins, so the film-makers wanted to make sure his features reflected his sad history.

A Sickly Dragon

The Ukrainian Ironbelly needed to have rusty scars from being held in chains. His colouring is a sickly white, and he is almost blind, the result of living in the dark vaults for many years. He hasn't been fed very well, so he's also very skinny and unhealthy.

To create the furious Ukrainian Ironbelly in CGI, the visual artists first created his skeleton and then layered a muscle frame on top of it. Digital animation helped the muscles deform, inflate and deflate the skin. Special tendons in the neck, shoulders and hips of the Ironbelly helped create more motion control and realistic movements for the reptile.

THREE OTHER IMPORTANT DRAGONS

The Triwizard Tournament introduced filmgoers to several other dragons as well. The Common Welsh Green is the smaller, smooth-scaled creature selected by Fleur Delacour (played by Clémence Poésy). The Chinese Fireball, selected by Viktor Krum (Stanislav Ianevski), is a red dragon with fine gold spikes around its face and large bat-like wings sprouting from its agile body. Cedric Diggory (Robert Pattinson), the first champion for Hogwarts, wound up with the Swedish Short-Snout dragon. This dragon stands out from the rest thanks to its resemblance to an alien or prehistoric monster.

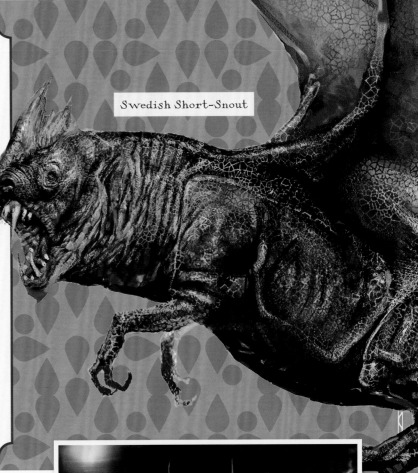

Swedish Short-Snout

Common Welsh Green

Chinese Fireball

Common Welsh Green

IN CLASS

CORNISH PIXIES

How can anyone forget those mischievous, giant-eared flying creatures known as Cornish pixies? First seen in the classroom of Professor Lockhart (Kenneth Branagh) during his Defence Against the Dark Arts class in *Harry Potter and the Chamber of Secrets*, the troublemaking, twenty-centimetre-tall creatures show up again in the Room of Requirement in *Harry Potter and the Deathly Hallows – Part 2*.

To create the impish pixies, the film's craftspeople built a scale model and painted it electric blue. The model was then cyberscanned and animated.

Left Hanging

In one of their memorable scenes, two pixies pull Neville Longbottom (played by Matthew Lewis) by the ears and hang him from a chandelier. To make the scene believable, Matthew had clips put behind his ears to push them up, as if the pixies were yanking on them.

Not all of the pixies' effects were computer-generated. Practical effects (thin wires) were used for the scenes in which the creatures pulled books off shelves and yanked students' hair.

Boggart

Nobody knows the true shape of a Boggart because it takes the form of a person's biggest fear. It appears as a cobra, a giant spider, and even as Professor Snape (actor Alan Rickman) in *Harry Potter and the Prisoner of Azkaban*.

Riddikulus!

Professor Remus Lupin (actor David Thewlis) points out in the movie, "Nobody knows what a Boggart looks like when he is alone, but when I let him out he will immediately become whatever each one of us most fears." Lupin teaches his third-year students how to cast the Riddikulus charm, which drives away the Boggart by changing it into something less fearsome.

From Screams to Laughter

The CGI helped deliver smooth, swirling transitions from the scary images to the comic versions of the Boggart for the sequences, like when Neville casts the Riddikulus charm to dress the Boggart impersonating Professor Snape in his grandmother's clothes.

Fearful Things

Ron uses the Riddikulus charm to put roller skates on an Acromantula, while Parvati (Sitara Shah) transforms a cobra into a jack-in-the-box. For Harry, the Boggart appears as a Dementor. Professor Lupin's worst fear is a full moon in the dark sky, which he turns into a white balloon. The film's visual effects artists created all this magic using digital images and computer effects.

COMPANIONS

Hedwig

From the minute the snowy owl made its first appearance in *Harry Potter and the Philosopher's Stone*, viewers knew that Hedwig was no ordinary bird. The beautiful feathered friend, which was given to Harry by Hagrid as a present on his eleventh birthday, is the perfect messenger.

Giving Lots of Hoots

Although Hedwig is a female owl, the part was played by several male snowy owls. That's because female owls are larger and have darker markings than male owls, so filming was easier with the males. A talented male owl named Gizmo did most of the work on the movie, while others called Kasper, Ook, Swoops, Oh Oh, Elmo and Bandit also played the part in the various Harry Potter movies.

Daniel Radcliffe wore a special protective leather arm guard, like the ones used by professional falconers, to work with Gizmo.

The film-makers used stand-ins for the live owl when they were preparing the lighting for flying sequences.

Broom-carrying Skills

In one of Hedwig's most challenging scenes, the owl presents Harry with a Nimbus 2000. Gizmo's handlers had to practise the scene with the bird for about six months to get him to carry the broom. The broom was made of plastic tubing, which is lighter than what owls usually carry in their claws. It was held by temporary attachments to his talons. Like the other Owl Post deliveries in the movie, the broom was tied to a harness mechanism released by the trainer so that Daniel Radcliffe could easily catch it.

Caring for Animal Performers

While many of the animals that appear in the Harry Potter films are digital creations or animatronic models, the film-makers occasionally used live owls, mice, cats, dogs, pigs, horses, crows and ravens to portray the creatures and animals of the wizarding world. The well-being and comfort of these animals was always a top priority. They were trained by professionals who cared for their safety and they were only kept on the set for short periods of time. Even the rats that are briefly seen scurrying inside a dark tunnel in *Harry Potter and the Chamber of Secrets* were treated to peanut butter to keep them happy and motivated!

Errol

A wonderful comic contrast to the brilliant Hedwig, Errol is the Weasley family's great grey owl. Played by an owl named Zeus, Errol is always causing little accidents, like slamming into windows. He even knocks over a bowl of crisps when he brings a Howler to Ron Weasley at Hogwarts.

Learning New Tricks

The animal trainers had a lot of fun putting together the scenes featuring Errol. After training the owl to fly with an envelope in his beak for *Harry Potter and the Chamber of Secrets*, they trained him how to lie down and get back up.

Handle with Care

Because owls have fragile, hollow bones, Zeus couldn't be filmed actually smashing into things, so when we see Errol colliding with the window in the movie, it's actually the result of digital computer effects and an animatronic version of the owl created by the creature shop.

PIGWIDGEON

The tiny owl Pigwidgeon was given to Ron by his family to replace his beloved pet rat, Scabbers. He didn't make his official film debut until *Harry Potter and the Half-Blood Prince*. Played by a beautiful scops owl named Mars, the tiny bird can often be found perched on a chair in the Gryffindor Common Room.

SCABBERS

Ron Weasley's pet rat, which was handed down to him by his brother Percy (Chris Rankin), appeared in *Harry Potter and the Philosopher's Stone*, *Harry Potter and the Chamber of Secrets* and *Harry Potter and the Prisoner of Azkaban* (as Peter Pettigrew's Animagus form).

Dex, the Star Rat

Scabbers was played by twelve real and several animatronic rats through the three movies. However, the most screen time went to a rat named Dex, who was trained to run and stay on mark.

Caught in the Sweet Box

An animatronic rat was used for a scene in which Scabbers gets his head caught in a sweet box. Dex joined the fun when the rat had to back out of the sweet box and end up sitting on Ron's lap. A trainer put a sweet box attached to a wire over Dex's head and gently pulled it off on cue.

Best Friends Forever

For the opening scene in *Harry Potter and the Prisoner of Azkaban*, Dex had to run down the hallway while being chased by Crackerjack, the cat that played Crookshanks. It took almost four months to train the animals to run in the same direction. The big challenge was that the cat would often catch up with the rat, because Dex wasn't afraid and wasn't running as fast as rats normally do! The two animals had really gotten used to each other's company.

CROOKSHANKS

Hermione's fluffy ginger cat made his film debut in *Harry Potter and the Prisoner of Azkaban*. The mischievous feline was often played by a male red Persian cat named Crackerjack.

Lots of Fur and Angry Eyes

Crackerjack's coat was created with "fur extensions", brushed-out undercoat fur that was clipped onto the cat's real fur by the trainers. To create the illusion of runny eyes, a clear, sting-free jelly-like substance was applied around his eyes. An animal-safe brown "eye shadow" was also painted around his eyes and mouth to make him look angry.

Getting an Earful

For a scene in *Harry Potter and the Order of the Phoenix*, Crookshanks had to yank at an Extendable Ear dangled by Fred and George Weasley (actors James and Oliver Phelps) over the staircase at number twelve, Grimmauld Place. It took trainers three months to teach Crackerjack (and two other cats, Prince and Pumpkin, who also subbed as Crookshanks) how to play with the ear, take it away, and drop it in a bowl off camera. Once the cats managed to perform the trick correctly, they were rewarded with a delicious kitty treat.

MRS NORRIS

Mrs Norris, the feline companion of Hogwarts caretaker Argus Filch, makes appearances in all eight of the Harry Potter movies. The sneaky cat, which seems to have a knack for catching misbehaving students and alerting Filch, was played by three Maine Coon cats named Maximus, Alanis and Tommy. Occasionally, the film-makers used an animatronic cat to fill in parts of the performance.

◆ The Perfect Pet ◆

Actor David Bradley, who played Filch in the movies, had a wonderful relationship with Maximus. The cat loved to jump on his back, sit on his shoulder and rest in his arms for hours.

FANG

Rubeus Hagrid's giant Neapolitan Mastiff, Fang, is known for his gentle and slightly cowardly nature. Fang was played by a Mastiff named Hugo from *Harry Potter and the Philosopher's Stone* through to *Harry Potter and the Prisoner of Azkaban*. Monkey played the role in *Harry Potter and the Goblet of Fire* and *Harry Potter and the Order of the Phoenix*, while Uno picked up the part in *Harry Potter and the Half-Blood Prince*. Other dogs – Bella, Vito, and Bully – also played Fang in the series.

Bully, a rescue dog, was adopted by one of the trainers when filming was completed.

Riding and Drooling

An animatronic version of Fang was created for the important scene in which the Ford Anglia car races out of the Forbidden Forest in *Harry Potter and the Chamber of Secrets*. The animatronic Mastiff was made to move and drool via a radio-controlled device.

Chewing Up the Scene

In *Harry Potter and the Order of the Phoenix*, Monkey had to catch a piece of steak and chew on it – a scene he probably enjoyed rehearsing more than anything else in his career. All the dogs were also trained to sit, stay, speak and come when directed to do so by trainers off camera.

Arnold

Ginny Weasley (Bonnie Wright) has a pink Pygmy Puff who made its screen debut in *Harry Potter and the Half-Blood Prince*. The magical creature was purchased at Ginny's twin brothers' shop, Weasleys' Wizard Wheezes. The blue-eyed Pygmy enjoys sitting on Ginny's shoulder as she shows it to Dean Thomas (actor Alfred Enoch) on the Hogwarts Express.

NO HAIR   HAIR

Pink Power

The creature designers came up with different looks for the small digital mammal, one with its characteristic pink fluffy hair and one without. Eventually, they decided to go with the version with the massively puffed hair.

TREVOR

In *Harry Potter and the Philosopher's Stone*, Neville Longbottom brings Trevor, his pet toad, along with him to Hogwarts. Not surprisingly, he ends up losing Trevor and creates havoc in the Gryffindor Common Room.

The toads were kept in a warm, moss-lined terrarium, and they were returned to their home right after their scene was shot.

◇ A Princely Toad ◇

Four different toads had the honour of playing Trevor in the series (he also appears in *Harry Potter and the Prisoner of Azkaban* and *Harry Potter and the Half-Blood Prince*). A trainer would always be ready to bring the toad to Matthew Lewis and put him in his hands, or gently rest him on the arm of a chair or on the floor as the scene required.

Fawkes

Harry Potter meets Fawkes the phoenix for the first time in Dumbledore's office in *Harry Potter and the Chamber of Secrets*, just before the ageing bird bursts into flames and emerges from the ashes as a newborn chick. The mythical birds are said to be immortal, and their magical tears have the ability to heal. Fawkes also brings Harry the Sorting Hat, which holds the Sword of Gryffindor, when he flies to Harry's aid in the Chamber of Secrets.

Ageing Before Our Eyes

The creature designers were tasked with visualizing various versions of the phoenix in different stages of its life – as the frail old bird, as the newborn chick, and as the powerful giant bird that helps Harry fight the Basilisk in the Chamber of Secrets. The concept artists looked at images of phoenixes in classical artwork and studied a variety of birds – especially sea eagles and vultures – for inspiration.

The newborn and the older, weakened versions of the bird look more like vultures, as they have stretched–out necks and layered wrinkles.

The animatronic Fawkes looked so realistic that the late actor Richard Harris (Dumbledore) thought it was actually a live, trained bird when he saw it for the first time.

The phoenix helps cure Harry Potter with his tears after he is wounded by the Basilisk and carries Harry, Ron, Ginny and Professor Lockhart out of the Chamber.

All the Right Details

The creature designers gave Fawkes a sharp beak and powerful claws to make him look a bit dangerous. To come up with the right textures and colouring for the bird, the designers went searching for a wide variety of pheasant feathers. In the end, they decided to go with a striking mixture of burnt-orange and dark-red feathers. For the baby Fawkes, they came up with a mix of washed-out pinkish-red and the grey colour of the ashes from which he emerges.

Tears of a Bird

The creature shop team crafted the large phoenix as an animatronic creature and in digital form. The animatronic version could slide on his perch, react to the other characters, and stretch his crimson wings to their full width. In addition, this animatronic version could actually cry the tears that were needed in the scene in which he helps heal Harry Potter's wounds after the attack by the Basilisk.

Taking Cues from Nature

Unlike many of the other creatures in the series, the digital version of Fawkes did not begin as a maquette or model that was then cyberscanned. The design team worked with the visual effects team to create the completely computer-generated Fawkes. They observed and filmed a turkey vulture and a blue macaw as reference. The midlife versions of Fawkes in *Harry Potter and the Goblet of Fire*, *Harry Potter and the Order of the Phoenix*, and *Harry Potter and the Half-Blood Prince* are all digital creations.

NAGINI

Nagini, the large and vicious snake companion of Lord Voldemort (Ralph Fiennes), is featured in some of the scariest scenes in *Harry Potter and the Order of the Phoenix* and *Harry Potter and the Deathly Hallows – Part 1* and *Part 2*. The slithering reptile, which is also a Horcrux, tries to kill Arthur Weasley in the Ministry of Magic headquarters, attempts to kill Harry Potter at Godric's Hollow, and is killed by Neville Longbottom in the final chapter of the series.

A Long and Slithering Serpent

The Nagini that appears in Harry's visions in *Harry Potter and the Goblet of Fire* was about six metres long and was conceived as a mixture of python and anaconda breeds. The creature shop artists made a full-scale model that was painted and cyberscanned. The same model was also used in *Harry Potter and the Order of the Phoenix*.

Bigger and Scarier

The Nagini seen in the last two films is a much bigger and more threatening creature. The digital artists studied a live python up close, sketching and recording sharp images of the reptile's scales. They used these details to add new shiny textures and reflective colours to the snake's skin. They also added physical characteristics of cobras and vipers to Nagini. If you look at her face carefully, you may recognize the brows, eyes and fangs associated with vipers.

Nagini bursts out of the body of Bathilda Bagshot in a suspenseful sequence in *Harry Potter and the Deathly Hallows – Part 1*. The visual effects artists used a mixture of live–action shots and the digital versions of Bathilda (actress Hazel Douglas) and Harry.

Don't Mess with Harry

To create the scene where Harry fights Nagini in the series finale, the film-makers combined live-action shots of Daniel Radcliffe fighting against crew members who were wearing green-screen gloves and holding him down. The crew were then digitally removed in postproduction, and Nagini was added to the final shots of the sequence.

THE WORKING WORLD

House-Elves

In the Harry Potter world, house-elves are obligated to serve one wizarding family for their entire lives. Although they have powerful magical abilities, they can only be released from their life of service if their master gives them an article of clothing as a gift. The two main house-elves featured in the film series are Dobby and Kreacher, who have very different temperaments and physical qualities.

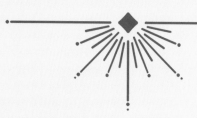

KREACHER

Kreacher is the house-elf who serves the Black family. Harry Potter meets the curmudgeon when he's taken to number twelve, Grimmauld Place in *Harry Potter and the Order of the Phoenix*. In *Harry Potter and the Deathly Hallows – Part 1*, Kreacher helps Harry find the real Horcrux locket.

DOBBY

We are first introduced to Dobby, the house-elf of the Malfoy family, in *Harry Potter and the Chamber of Secrets*. He becomes Harry's loyal friend after Harry finds a way to save him from a life of servitude under the Malfoys. Dobby was the first fully computer-generated major character of the Harry Potter movies. A much-loved and endearing creature, Dobby went through many design changes until the creative team zeroed in on the final version, which has soulful green eyes, large bat-like ears, and that unforgettable pointy nose.

A Rough Life

Dobby has been serving the Malfoys for many years when he meets Harry, so the designers decided to give him a pasty, sickly appearance to reflect his tough life. His skin had to be a bit dirty and his body would be weak, with very little muscle tone. The creature shop created a full-size, fully articulated and painted silicone model to stand in for lighting reference and for actors to establish their eyelines. The silicone model was also used for some over-the-shoulder shots in the movie.

S.P.E.W.

SOCIETY FOR THE PROMOTION OF ELFISH WELFARE

GOBLINS

The goblins featured in the Harry Potter series work as bank officials and tellers at Gringotts Wizarding Bank in Diagon Alley. They have long fingers, giant ears and long noses, and their personalities are reflected heavily in their appearance. Each goblin's ears, chin and nose were individually designed.

Better Prosthetics

The prosthetic pieces used to create the goblins' faces improved a lot in the ten-year period between the two movies in which they appear. The goblins' heads for both movies were made out of silicone, but the new and improved version of the material moves freely and feels more like flesh.

The Bank Job

More than sixty goblins were created for the bank scene in *Harry Potter and the Deathly Hallows – Part 2*, so the creature shop had a large team of technicians to paint goblin faces and hands and insert hair and eyelashes one strand at a time.

Griphook

The goblin Griphook made his first appearance in *Harry Potter and the Philosopher's Stone*, in which he guides Harry to the Potter family vault. He shows up again in *Harry Potter and the Deathly Hallows – Part 2*, when he agrees to help Harry break into the Lestranges' vault.

The goblin prosthetics couldn't be reused after they were removed at the end of the day, so several versions of each goblin head were created, enough to cover every day of filming.

Tough Transformation

It took veteran actor Warwick Davis four hours to transform into Griphook. He had to wear prosthetics as well as special contact lenses and dentures with very sharp teeth. It took another hour after the filming was done to remove the make-up. In *Harry Potter and the Philosopher's Stone*, Griphook was physically played by Verne Troyer, but was voiced by Davis.

DARK FORCES

Basilisk

We encounter the deadly reptile known as the Basilisk in *Harry Potter and the Chamber of Secrets*. The slithering creature that lives deep below Hogwarts is released during the events of the movie. It's up to Harry to kill it and save the school. The Basilisk's skeleton is seen in *Harry Potter and the Deathly Hallows – Part 2*, when Ron and Hermione journey into the Chamber of Secrets to destroy Helga Hufflepuff's cup.

Rubber Snakeskin

From the start, the plan was to create the Basilisk digitally using computer-generated imagery. So a realistic model was produced to be cyberscanned. In addition, the film-makers needed a prop of the Basilisk's shed skin in the Chamber of Secrets. The creature shop artists created the first twelve metres of discarded snakeskin out of rubber.

Fangs for the Memories

It was later decided that a full-size practical version of the Basilisk was needed for the scene where Harry is fighting the monster. This realistic model of the head needed to extend as far as the neck, and it also required a fully moving lower jaw as well as a nose, mouth, eyes and eyelids. Its fangs had to hinge backward so that it could close its mouth!

A Python Named Doris

The Basilisk's head is shaped like a dragon and its body is bony and thorny. To create the venomous creature, the visual effects artists observed several live reptiles, including a two-metre-long Burmese python named Doris.

Dementors

The Dark, soul-sucking creatures that haunt Harry Potter and are sent to Hogwarts to find and bring back Sirius Black were first seen in *Harry Potter and the Prisoner of Azkaban*. They also attack Harry and Dudley Dursley (Harry Melling) in Little Whinging in *Harry Potter and the Order of the Phoenix* and fight on Voldemort's side in the last two films.

Floating Fabrics in the Air

Because Dementors are insubstantial creatures with very little visible structure, the visual effects artists came up with a veiled, skeletal shape that could glide in the air. They wrapped them in shroud-like black robes that hang from their skulls. The costume department put together an assortment of fabrics that emphasized the floating effect.

Underwater Puppets

Since the Dementors do not speak, creating the right movements for them was important for the movie magic to work. The visual effects team originally looked at fabric-covered Dementor models, using different wind and lighting effects. They even asked a world-renowned puppeteer to test the models floating underwater and ran the film backwards and in slow motion. But the process was too difficult to pull off, so they used the filmed footage as a starting point to create the Dementors via CGI.

The designers looked at ancient embalmed bodies with rotting wrappings and added textures to give the Dementors a special decaying effect.

Revealing More Details

A different approach was taken for depicting the Dementors in the later movies. In *Harry Potter and the Order of the Phoenix*, their hoods were removed and their robes were drawn back, revealing more of their bodies and facial features.

Strong Arms

The Dementors also needed powerful arms and articulated hands to hold Harry up against the underpass wall. At first, the designers planned to reimagine the hanging strips of the shrouds to act as limbs (like an octopus's arms). But it didn't look right for these creatures to have so many arms. In the final version, their creepy hands have a more human look.

Inferi

✦ ✦

The resurrected corpses that are brought back to life by Dark wizards are unique creatures in the Harry Potter world. We see them for the first time in *Harry Potter and the Half-Blood Prince* when Harry and Dumbledore (Michael Gambon) are trying to enter a sea cave to retrieve the Slytherin locket. They are blocked by the reanimated forces of the skeleton-like Inferi.

The Living Dead
Woodcuts from the Middle Ages, as well as visuals from classics such as *Paradise Lost* and Dante's *Inferno*, helped inspire the frightening look of these reanimated dead creatures.

The visual effects team used new software that helped them create a large number of Inferi interacting with water and with the flames of the firestorm that ends the big confrontation.

Grey, Black and Digital

Because it was determined that the Inferi had to be computer-generated creatures, a male and female version were sculpted at full size and then cyberscanned. The creatures were painted at a later stage via computer, using tones of grey and black. A texture was also added to give the impression that they were once covered with flesh.

Harry in the Tank

The film-makers didn't want the Inferi to look too much like zombies. They filmed a group of men and women coming out of a lake and used motion-capture technology to add their facial and bodily movements to the digital creatures. The digital Inferi were then added to film footage of Harry in a water tank as he was being dragged underwater and embraced by a female Inferius.

ISBN 978-1-4063-7702-6

Published 2017 by
Walker Books Ltd
87 Vauxhall Walk
London SE11 5HJ

www.walker.co.uk

Produced by

PO Box 3088
San Rafael, CA 94912
www.insighteditions.com

Publisher: Raoul Goff
Co-publisher: Michael Madden
Executive Editor: Vanessa Lopez
Art Director: Chrissy Kwasnik
Design and Layout: Ashley Quackenbush and Leah Bloise
Project Editor: Greg Solano
Managing Editor: Alan Kaplan
Production Editor: Rachel Anderson
Production Managers: Thomas Chung, Alix Nicholaeff, and Lina sp Temena
Production Coordinator: Leeana Diaz
Production Assistant: Sam Taylor

REPLANTED PAPER

Insight Editions, in association with Roots of Peace, will plant two trees for each tree
used in the manufacturing of this book. Roots of Peace is an internationally renowned
humanitarian organization dedicated to eradicating land mines worldwide and
converting war-torn lands into productive farms and wildlife habitats. Roots of Peace
will plant two million fruit and nut trees in Afghanistan and provide farmers there with
the skills and support necessary for sustainable land use.

Manufactured in Shenzhen, China, by Insight Editions

20177026R0
10 9 8 7 6 5 4 3 2 1